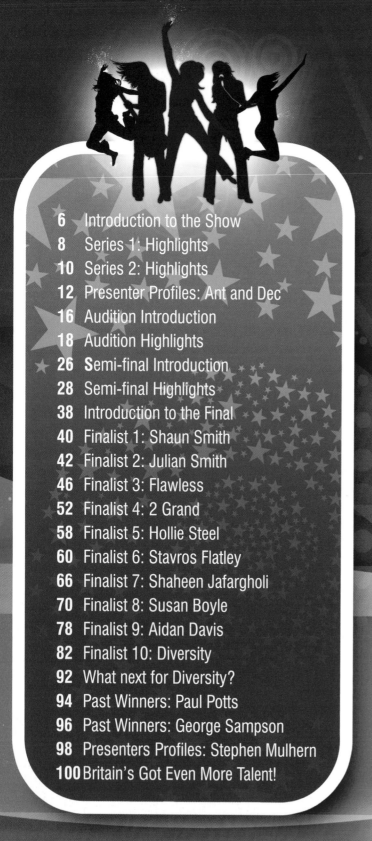

Written by Rachel Elliot.
Published 2009. Pedigree Books, Beech Hill House,
Walnut Gardens, Exeter, Devon, EX4 4DH.
books@pedigreegroup.co.uk • www.pedigreebooks.com

BRITAIN'S GOT T★LENT

£7.99

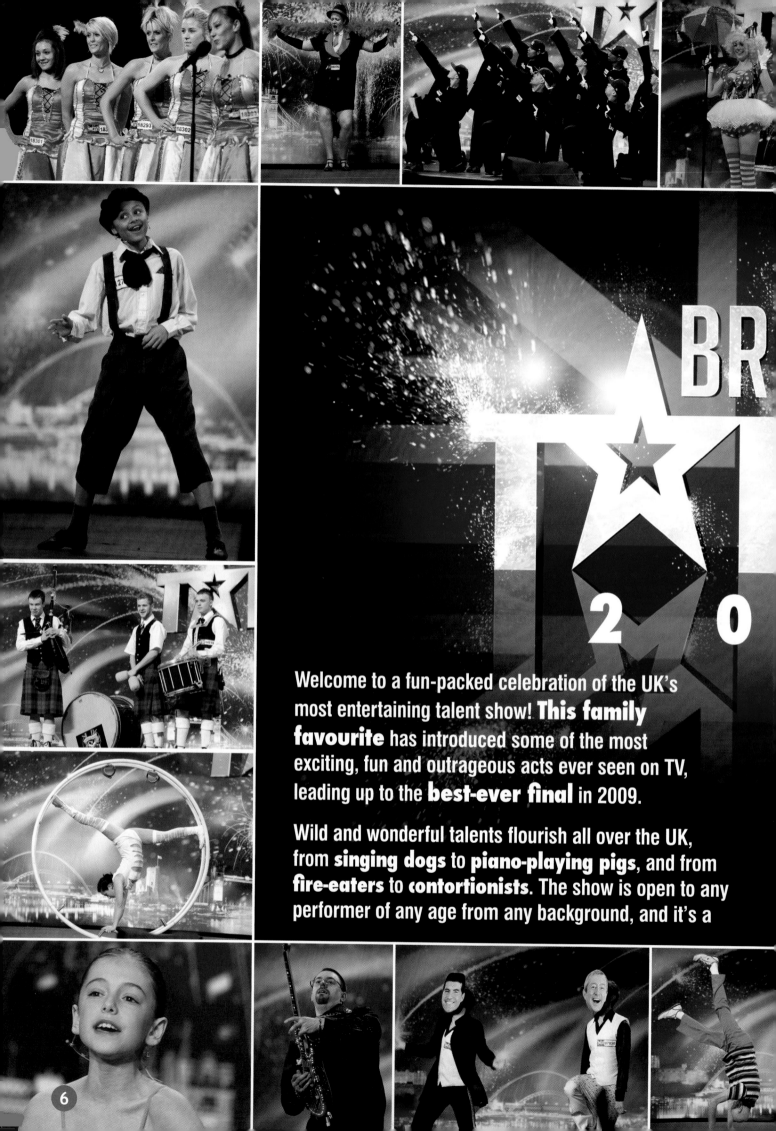

BR ☆ **2 0**

Welcome to a fun-packed celebration of the UK's most entertaining talent show! **This family favourite** has introduced some of the most exciting, fun and outrageous acts ever seen on TV, leading up to the **best-ever final** in 2009.

Wild and wonderful talents flourish all over the UK, from **singing dogs** to **piano-playing pigs**, and from **fire-eaters** to **contortionists**. The show is open to any performer of any age from any background, and it's a

ΑΙΝ'S GOT ΕΝΤ

0 9

place where dreams really can come true. The fantastic reward awaiting the winner is an appearance on the Royal Variety Performance and £100,000 prize money.

Track the progress of your favourite performers through the auditions and semi-finals, remind yourself of the best moments and the most **memorable acts**, judge the Judges and explore the background stories of all the finalists. Enjoy the spectacular final all over again, and remember – Britain's definitely got **talent**!

SERIES 1

A little girl with an angelic voice – Connie Talbot delighted everyone with her astonishing singing talent.

Victoria Armstrong made sure the Judges would never think of angle grinders in the same way!

Comedian Jake Pratt held the audience in the palm of his hand!

Series one burst onto our screens in 2007, and audiences went wild with excitement. Do you remember these magical moments?

The Mini Mezzos fizzed with energy!

Luke and Charlotte burned up the stage with their dynamic footwork!

Crazee Horse – the breathtaking husband-and-wife balancing act.

Damon Scott astonished everyone with his miming monkey!

SERIES 2

Female string quartet Escala were as electric as their instruments!

Martial-arts demonstration team Strike gave a dramatic audition!

Signature's unique dance act was an instant hit and their outstanding performance led them straight to the final!

Series two was bigger, brighter and even better than series one. Which was your favourite performance of the series?

These energetic Cheeky Monkeys were infectiously entertaining!

Simon was bowled over by Charlie Green's fresh voice.

Kate and Gin's incredible routines and special bond gained them a standing ovation and the affection of a nation!

Faryl Smith's huge voice captivated the audience.

ANT M^cPARTLIN DECLAN DONNELLY

Ant and Dec met on the set of hit TV show *Byker Grove* when they were thirteen years old. They formed a strong bond and have been best friends ever since. Since those early days they have worked together on a huge variety of TV shows, including *SMTV Live, CD:UK, I'm a Celebrity . . . Get Me Out of Here!, Ant & Dec's Saturday Night Takeaway* and *Pop Idol*.

The lads seem able to turn their hands to anything, and their enthusiasm and enjoyment are infectious. Above all, their true friendship shines through on screen. They are British entertainment royalty, and that makes them the perfect hosts for *Britain's Got Talent*!

"I want to be Greek!" – Ant after seeing Stavros Flatley perform.

"That was brilliant!" Dec on Ben and Becky's dancing.

Their many awards include the Special Recognition Award at the National Television Awards for their contribution to television, and Most Popular Entertainment Presenters at the National Television Awards for the last eight years in a row.

FACT FILE

Birthday: November 18th, 1975

Full name: Anthony David McPartlin

Favourite football team: Newcastle United

How to recognise him: Ant usually stands on the left of the screen!

"You didn't expect that did you? Did you? No!" – Ant on Susan Boyle's first audition.

FACT FILE

Birthday: September 25th, 1975

Full name: Declan Joseph Oliver Donnelly

Favourite football team: Newcastle United

How to recognise him: Dec usually stands on the right of the screen!

DID YOU KNOW?

★ Dec is the youngest of seven children.

★ Ant first appeared on TV on children's programme *Why Don't You*.

★ Dec's favourite Newcastle player is Alan Shearer.

★ Ant and Dec are keen Newcastle United fans.

★ Dec's first TV appearance was on the set of *Byker Grove*.

★ Ant's favourite film is *Die Hard*.

★ After signing a record contract in 1993, Ant and Dec had fourteen Top Twenty hits and three multi-platinum albums.

For Ant and Dec, series three was the most exciting yet. It was bigger and better than ever before, and they really enjoyed meeting the wacky and wonderful contestants as they waited for their big chance in front of the Judges. They love the feel-good atmosphere of the show, and the fact that it's a real celebration of raw talent. Check out their series highlights!

Ant annoyed Darth Jackson when he tried to take his lightsaber!

"She's got them on their feet out there!" – Dec

DJ Talent had and Dec danci the wings!

"He can't believe it, look! Never done anything like this before, and he gets a reception like that!" – Ant

"Could she be any cuter?" – Ant

THE AUDITIONS

It's the first stage of *Britain's Got Talent* 2009 – the auditions!

The atmosphere is electric as the audience arrives, buzzing with anticipation. Anyone could walk onto that stage. Will it be a dazzling dancer? A spectacular singer? A mystifying magician? Will they see the winner's first audition? Right now, anything is possible.

The hum rises to a roar of applause as the Judges arrive! Amanda directs a dazzling smile at the audience, looking effortlessly glamorous. Simon gives a relaxed smile and waves, looking delighted to be back on *Britain's Got Talent*. Piers shoots a wry smile at the crowd, his eyes sparkling. Fans call out to their favourite judge as all three step up to their desk, where three red buzzers are waiting.

Now a hush falls over the crowd. The acts are waiting backstage, ready to audition. Their nerves have reached fever pitch! Knees are trembling and hearts are hammering with anticipation.

Emotions are running high. Some people have arrived with friends and family to support them. Others sit alone, quietly running through their routines one last time. Some are brimming with confidence while others drum their fingers anxiously and bite their lips.

There are people here from all walks of life. Old or young, big or small, extrovert or shy, anyone can make it if they have the talent! Ant and Dec move among the nervous acts, asking them where they're from... and trying to relax them with a few jokes!

At last the moment has arrived. The Judges are ready, the audience is breathless with excitement, and the first act steps nervously onto the stage.

Britain's Got Talent 2009 has begun!

SIMON

AM

The Paws For Thought display team was dog chaos. Fire brought the auditions to a standstill, but Ant stepped in and put the flames out!

Not even a talking toucan could wow the Judges!

From cheeky chicks...

"Your snakes are too small."

...to dancing dragons!

Humans are not the only ones with talent! What did you think of these brilliant beasts?

Carriad's act didn't go as planned, but she had lots of fun waving the Welsh flag in front of Simon!

Do you remember these pretty penguins?

Happy Harry wasn't so happy during his audition – he had an attack of stage fright and didn't make a sound!

The Dog Positive Posse went for walkies onstage... but they got three buzzers from the Judges.

"It's three moos."

19

SIMON   AM

Who could forget Knit and Natter in an attempt to teach the audience to finger knit? The Judges' faces told the whole story!

What A Palaver's outrageous act found a new use for handbags!

"OK, it's not as easy as it looks!"

Mr Methane tried to sing with his bottom. He adopted the farting position, but Simon was not amused!

Happy acts make happy Judges – and sometimes the most unexpected things happen onstage!

Dan Kahn's act made Simon and Amanda cringe, but Piers refused to buzz him!

Mike Henderson made everyone feel nervous – especially when Piers buzzed him at a crucial moment and he nearly became a sword swallower!

Flippin Bonkers is the sort of act that cheers everyone up. They got a yes from each judge – Amanda appreciated the message on Adam's chest!

The Judges have to face some hairy, scary acts!

"Oh Mr Scowl, I feel dizzy!"

James Boyd was hoping to get into the Guinness Book of Records by eating the most chocolates he could in one minute. Ant and Dec tried to match him backstage – and Ant actually beat him!

Wild Wayne Moseley's super-loud drumming couldn't beat him a path to the semi-final.

Some people have a *burning* ambition to be famous!

Street performer Adrian Pirate rode onto the stage on a motorbike to grab the attention of the Judges!

I thought it was brilliant!"

29751

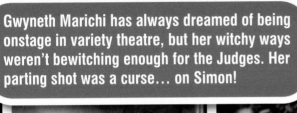

PIERS

Some of the acts seem to genuinely scare the Judges, but among even the worst audition days there are some shining lights.

Gwyneth Marichi has always dreamed of being onstage in variety theatre, but her witchy ways weren't bewitching enough for the Judges. Her parting shot was a curse... on Simon!

David Darbyshire's chainsaw antics were a hit with the Judges.

The judges didn't think that Pavabotti's performance would impress the Queen!

WALK THRU A WALL

Amazing Steve failed to amaze the audience.

"I'm going to do break dancing."

"What's he going to break?"

Family group Good Evans sang *I'll Be There* and had the audience on their feet!

SIMON | AM

Singing Souls wanted to show the Judges what it takes to win *Britain's Got Talent*. The Judges just wanted them to leave the stage...

Daiquiri Dusk performed a traditional Scottish dance... with a twist.

Simon said Bonnee Rox's act was like putting a wolf and a hamster in the same cage.

Lee Patey's off his trolley!

Izabella thought the Queen would want to watch an aerobics lesson. Piers thought not

The auditions are a time to celebrate for some...

Ray Brooke played his walking stick with pride.

Betty Delight clowned around!

Me and My Shadow: Andy and Ben, the smoothest used-car dealers in the UK, had everyone singing along!

Frankie Siragusa's belly dancing mesmerised Simon!

"I'm the old man's Gene Kelly."

Direct from London, it's time for the *Britain's Got Talent* semi-finals!

The first audition stages have been completed, and the forty semi-final acts have been chosen. If the atmosphere backstage was tense before, it's skyrocketing now! After an incredible seven weeks, the audience takes over, and the acts will be battling for votes.

Even though it's the semi-finals, the Judges can still press their buzzers if they don't like an act. If the act gets three red crosses, the performance will be over. But now the viewers can vote for their favourites and help to decide which ten acts will go through to the final!

Hosts Ant and Dec are ready to guide the nervous acts and the cheering audience through a thrilling evening packed with talent. They welcome the three Judges onto the stage, and the crowd goes wild. But right now the Judges are just as excited as the audience. The viewer votes will send the top act through to the glittering final- with a further act voted through by the judges. So this is where the competition really starts.

"You have a huge amount of talent."

FACES OF DISCO

This comedy dance act began as a way of raising money at university. Best friends Rich and Liam are full of confidence and they want to win. But they will have to work out something completely new to prove that they can keep surprising the audience!

They pour energy, enthusiasm and humour into their semi-final performance – but is it enough to carry them forward to the final?

DARTH JACKSON

Darth Jackson is a postal worker by day, but ever since he was a child he has loved Darth Vader. He learned to sing and dance through the music of Michael Jackson, and he has chosen to combine his two passions in his act.

Although Simon Cowell is not a fan, Darth Jackson is a man with a mission. He desperately wants to prove Simon wrong, and make it through to the final. Darth Jackson's dark figure appears onstage with a backing of dancing storm troopers. He dances and the audience cheers, but has he done enough?

"I want to show the world what I can do!"

"Darth, I was feeling the Force tonight!"

HIGHLIGHTS

NATALIE OKRI

Ten-year-old Natalie Okri loves singing and is hugely excited to have made it through to the semi-finals. She wants to get the audience singing along with her, and hopes to show everyone how important music is in her life.

The music starts to play and Natalie walks confidently onto the stage.

She sings from the heart and throws her energy into her performance. Will she make it to the final?

"Nobody can imagine how much it means to me."

"You're one of the cutest kids I've ever seen."

SUE SON

Sue Son got her first violin when she was six, and her music is at the centre of her life. She originally came on to *Britain's Got Talent* as a duo with her friend Janine, but the Judges asked her to come back as a solo act. It was a difficult decision, but she chose to take her chance and has made it through to the semi-finals.

Looking stunning in a red dress, Sue Son steps onto the stage and plays her heart out, aiming for a place in the final.

Fire erupts around her as her music electrifies the studio audience. But will the public vote for her?

"You are a vixen with a violin."

THROUGH TO THE FINAL
Susan Boyle & Diversity

DJ TALENT

Rapper DJ Talent's trademark gold teeth are glittering as he grins in excitement. The bling is ready, the song is ready and the audience is ready. But no one could have expected him to emerge on a golden throne!

"I thought that was a very, very good performance."

"It was a musical nightmare."

GARETH OLIVER

Ventriloquist Gareth Oliver has been performing for ten years and feels that his performance on *Britain's Got Talent* is make or break. He has created a brand-new character, but will it be enough to win the hearts of the audience?

Gareth gives a wonderful performance with his opera-singing, joke-telling dummy. The audience loves him, but will the voting reflect that?

JAMIE PUGH

Jamie Pugh's first audition electrified the Judges. A shy, nervous man stepped onto the stage and made the audience erupt with his fantastic voice. But can he pull off the same feat with an audience of millions watching?

HIGHLIGHTS

MERLIN CADOGAN

The Judges asked escapologist Merlin for more danger, so that's exactly what he's going to give them. Merlin is tied into a straitjacket as he intends to escape from it while hanging upside down... from a burning rope!

HOT HONEYZ

Simon told the Hot Honeyz that "less is more" in their audition, so for the semi-final they are determined to impress him. Will they succeed?

THROUGH TO THE FINAL
Flawless & Shaun Smith

"I can't believe I'm in the semi-final!"

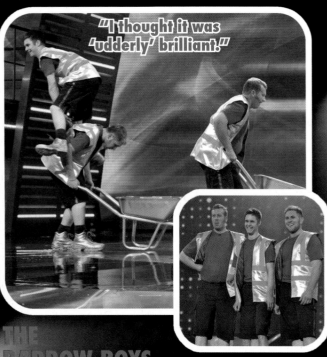

"I thought it was 'udderly' brilliant!"

THE BARROW BOYS

This farming threesome use their wheelbarrows to create a totally unique act that's very different from their day job. They have been practising in front of their cows, and have danced their way through over twenty wheelbarrows!

The Barrow Boys have customised their wheelbarrows to enable them to give a truly magical performance at the semi-final. They perform energetic and acrobatic feats, but both Piers and Simon buzz them before the end of the act!

"I thought that was a lot of fun."

"My act is fit for the queen."

HARMONY

The Harmony girls have spent all the spare time singing along to their favourite songs and dreaming of stardom. That dream seems so close they can almost touch it as they get ready to perform on *Britain's Got Talent*.

The act starts with a bang as the girls burst out of an enormous pink cake! Their infectious energy gets the audience on their feet.

HIGHLIGHTS

BEN & BECKY

This brother and sister ballroom-dancing act united the Judges in loving their audition – but can they raise their game for the semi-final? Their unique chemistry fills their performance with energy.

Ben and Becky throw all their enthusiasm and love of dancing into their act, and the audience erupts as they carry out spectacular lifts and super-tight moves. They just hope that it's enough to take them one step closer to their dream.

"Simon just doesn't appreciate beauty."

Their rawness lit up the stage at the auditions and everyone is looking forward to finding out what they are going to do next.

The audience squeals in excitement as the stage erupts and the group's raw energy explodes with a spectacular routine. No one has seen anything like it!

MD SHOWGROUP

MD Showgroup are a young dance troupe from Liverpool, determined to show that they have got what it takes to perform at the Royal Variety Performance.

"I wish I could bottle your passion!"

"Perfection – technically perfect."

THROUGH TO THE FINAL
Stavros Flatley & Shaheen Jafargholi

33

"Vocally it's just not there."

BRIT CHIX

The Brit Chix are bursting with enthusiasm and can't wait to get onto the semi-final stage to show the Judges and the audience what they can do. These cool, sassy girls want the chance to perform in front of the Queen – who they call the original Brit Chick!

However, the girls get a shock when they receive three buzzes from the Judges!

JACKIE PRESCOTT & TIPPY TOES

Jackie's dog is her best friend, and they both have an enormous amount of fun training for their act. During their audition, Simon suggested that Tippy Toes should try tap dancing, although Amanda and Piers thought it was a big mistake. However, Jackie and Tippy Toes had great fun.

Tippy Toes was nervous performing in front of such a big audience, but her delightful personality shone out and even charmed Mr Nasty himself!

"I've definitely got a few more tricks up my sleeve."

"She has really improved and she's cute."

HIGHLIGHTS

CALLUM FRANCIS

Twelve-year-old Callum hugely impressed the Judges with his audition. He can sing and dance, and his infectious charm was commented on by the Judges.

Callum's dream is to sing and dance onstage in the West End. The chance to perform on the Royal Variety Performance has set his imagination on fire. Can his Jungle Book routine improve on his audition performance?

"I'm so fit."

"I thought it was the perfect audition for you."

SUGARFREE

Sugarfree is made up of seven girls who share a single passion. They are best friends and they all love to dance. Through dedicated training they have achieved a chemistry and bond that seems unbreakable. But can their act stand up in the toughest category on the show? And what will the Judges say?

"You are the best girl dance group we've seen."

THROUGH TO THE FINAL
Julian Smith & 2 Grand

"Tonight I'm giving it everything I've got."

GREG PRITCHARD

Greg's high-pitched audition astonished, puzzled and delighted the Judges. Now he's back for the semi-final, and he's hugely excited! Singing is what he has wanted to do since the age of three, and this is his big chance. The stage is transformed by Greg's vast cloak and although Simon buzzes him he keeps going, until the audience erupts with applause. Greg feels satisfied that he has shown the Judges his full vocal range!

"I'm starting to question what this show is all about."

MARTIN MATCHAM

At Martin's audition, Simon said that he thought Martin could single-handedly close down the show. Martin got through to the semi-finals anyway, but his mother-in-law had a few words to say to Simon!

Martin plans to give the semi-finals everything he's got and light up the stage. Can he win Simon over?

HIGHLIGHTS

THE DREAMBEARS

By day these comedy dancers are three ordinary guys with ordinary jobs… but by night they are cabaret singers! They have pulled out all the stops for their semi-final performance. They drop down to the stage from above, and then launch themselves into an energetic routine that has the audience singing and dancing along with them. High kicks and acrobatics aren't enough for Simon, who buzzes them after just a few seconds!

"We've taken so many risks tonight!"

GOOD EVANS

The Evans are a very close family and love spending time together. In the audition, the Judges suggested that the parents should take a more behind-the-scenes role, but the family has decided that they want to perform together. It's obvious to the audience that they love being onstage, and everyone warmed to the strong family atmosphere – perfect for *Britain's Got Talent!*

"A lovely bit of credit crunch camp."

THROUGH TO THE FINAL
Hollie Steel & Aidan Davis

YOUR FINALISTS

It all comes down to this moment – ten acts battling it out for one coveted place at the Royal Variety Performance and £100,000 prize money! The British public have picked up the phone and voted for their favourites, and now the finalists are waiting to give the most important performance of their lives.

After thousands of auditions and five thrilling semi-finals, this is the biggest and most exciting final ever. Ten sensational acts can feel their dream within reach at last.

The *Britain's Got Talent* family is assembled. Ant and Dec are brimming with excitement – they can't wait to find out who will become the third

winner of *Britain's Got Talent*. The Judges walk onstage for the last show of the series, and the audience cheers wildly as Simon, Amanda and Piers take their positions.

The Judges are in place, the audience is ready and Ant and Dec are waiting to introduce the first act.

FLAWLESS

STAVROS FLATLEY

2 GRAND

JULIAN SMITH

SUSAN BOYLE

SHAUN SMITH

HOLLIE STEEL

SHAHEEN JAFARGHOLI

DIVERSITY

AIDAN DAVIS

After weeks of waiting, the moment of truth is almost here. The *Britain's Got Talent* final has begun!

Shaun Smith is seventeen and studying for his A-Levels at school, as well as being a star on the rugby pitch. But his real passion is singing, and he arrived at the first auditions hoping that he could put on a good show. He did better than that... he gave a spectacular performance that catapulted him all the way to the finals!

Audition

Song: *Ain't No Sunshine*

Judges' Reaction: Simon said, "I genuinely wasn't expecting that!" He added, "You've got a very authentic sounding voice and you didn't make that sound karaoke – I think you're really good." Piers and Amanda agreed with Simon, although Amanda did have one criticism about Shaun's nervous body language. She said, "Take your hands out of your pockets – believe in yourself!"

Verdict: Three yesses!

Shaun's Reaction: He was really nervous, and said that auditioning in front of the Judges was scary!

SHAUN SMITH

Semi-Final

Song: *With or Without You.*

Judges' Reaction: Piers said that when Shaun started singing, he wasn't sure it was the right song. But when Shaun hit the big note, and the audience erupted, all his doubts melted away. Amanda was brimming with delight because Shaun's confidence was shining through, and even Simon was smiling! He said, "That was a brilliant choice of song... that was terrific, well done!"

Verdict: The Judges chose to put Shaun through to the final.

Shaun's Reaction: Shaun was terrified, but determined to give his performance everything he'd got. After the fantastic comments from the Judges, he was on cloud nine!

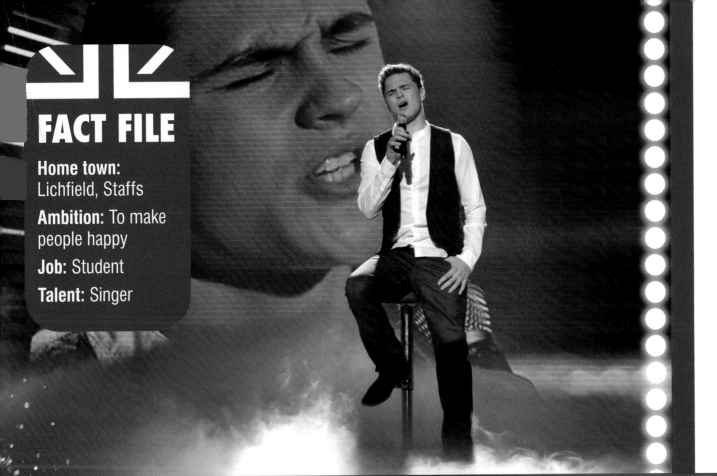

Home town:
Lichfield, Staffs

Ambition: To make
people happy

Job: Student

Talent: Singer

"I want this so badly, it hurts."

Final

In His Words: "I'm on top of the world about being in the final tonight; I couldn't feel any better. This has changed my life. I now know what I have to do with my life – I have to pursue this career."

Song: *Ain't No Sunshine.*

Judges' Reaction: Simon was full of praise, saying, "Shaun, you said you wanted to give the performance of your life, and guess what? You did. I thought you sang the song brilliantly." Piers agreed with Simon! But he also pointed out that Shaun was in a difficult category with some stunning singers, and the competition was tough. Amanda added, "You've ticked every box tonight... and you're right to think about pursuing this as a career in the future. Congratulations!"

Shaun's Reaction:
"It was so much fun – I enjoyed every second of it!"

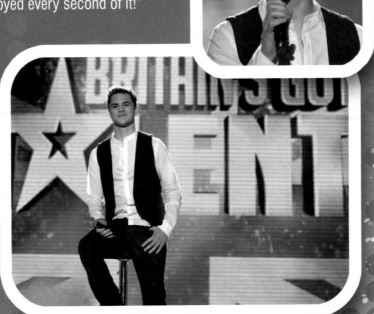

39-year-old Julian Smith has three loves in his life – his wife, his children . . . and his saxophone. He has always dreamed of using his musical talents to earn a living onstage. He hopes to be able to make life better for himself and his family, and to be able to tell his daughters that he followed his dream and succeeded.

Julian has been playing the saxophone since he was fourteen, but has never achieved the recognition he feels he deserves. He has performed at pubs and restaurants in and around Birmingham, but it is his dream to play larger arenas.

He is inspired by Kenny G and would love to be equally as well known.

Julian feels as if the story of his life is that he didn't quite make it. He has a great fear that it could happen again, but he is determined to do his best to impress the Judges and win the hearts of the nation with his music.

"This competition has given me a lifeline."

JULIAN SMITH

"Playing the saxophone is my life."

Audition

Song: Julian stood in the centre of the stage with his saxophone in his hand. It was the biggest audience that he had ever faced, and he was feeling very nervous. He lifted the saxophone to his mouth and began to play Somewhere from West Side Story.

Judges' Reaction: Julian's extraordinary talent held the audience spellbound. As the long, soaring last note echoed around the studio, the audience rose to their feet, cheering, clapping and whistling to show their delight. Amanda wiped tears from her eyes and said that it was "absolutely stunning". Piers added that he was blown away by the

emotion in Julian's playing. Simon looked Julian straight in the eyes. The audience held its breath. Had Simon liked the performance? Would he have something cutting to say? "The whole idea about doing this show is to find someone who needs a break but who's got a huge talent," said Simon. "I believe that we've found that with you. That was a beautiful choice of music. There could be something special about you."

Verdict: Three yesses!

Julian's Reaction: Julian was overwhelmed to be through to the next round!

"I feel like my whole life has led to this point."

42

FACT FILE

Home town:
Birmingham

Ambition: To play
the saxophone for
a living

Job: Music teacher

Talent: Saxophone
player

Semi-Final

Song: For the semi-final, Julian played All By Myself. Everyone was holding his or her breath, willing him to succeed. As he hit the high notes of the song, the audience erupted. Julian's confidence seemed to grow with every cheer, and at the end of the piece he thanked the audience for supporting him so warmly. Having faced so many disappointments in the past, he could hardly dare to believe that his chance might have come at last.

Judges' Reaction: The Judges were delighted with Julian's performance.

Verdict: At the end of the show, the audience voted Julian through to the final.

Julian's Reaction: Being voted through by the public made Julian feel as if people really did believe in him. He was delighted to be one step closer to his dream!

"Thank you for giving me this opportunity."

Final

In His Words: Julian knew that his dreams were riding on his performance, and he had to play better than he had ever played before if he was going to be in with a chance to win. He paced up and down as he waited for his turn to perform on one of the most important nights of his life.

Song: When Julian started to play Somewhere – the same tune he had played for his audition – he melted the hearts of the audience.

Judges' Reaction: The sound of the solo saxophone echoed through the studio, and as he hit the high notes, the Judges joined the audience in a standing ovation.

Julian's Reaction: Julian knew that he had given the performance of his life!

"To play the saxophone for a living would be the ultimate dream."

Flawless was formed four years ago by Marlon, the group's choreographer. They dream of inspiring children from problem communities to channel their aggression and energy into something positive. If they won the £100,000 prize money, they would like to open a centre where they could teach children and help build their confidence through dance.

The dance troupe rehearses every day and love dancing. It is their dream to perform in front of the Queen. Their energy and attitude embody the spirit of *Britain's Got Talent*. They show that if you're willing to work hard for your passion, you can achieve anything!

With their friends and family in the audience, they were ready to give the performance of their lives!

FLAWLESS

"Chase the dream, not the competition."

Audition

Act: Dressed in black-and-white suits and black hats, Flawless brought the audience to their feet with their stupendous audition performance. At the end, it seemed as if the applause would never stop!

"We love dancing!"

Judges' Reaction: The Judges were on their feet, cheering along with the audience. In the wings, Ant and Dec were equally excited. "It was utterly electrifying!" said Piers. "A jaw-droppingly outstanding performance." Amanda added.

Simon gave one of the best compliments of the series when he said, "This is one of the best things I've ever seen in my life."

Verdict: Simon said that they didn't just get three yesses, they got four thousand. The audience was right behind them!

Flawless's Reaction: The group raced offstage to hug their families, who were waiting with bated breath!

FACT FILE

Home town:
North London

Talent: Street dancing

Members:
Marlon Wallen 24,
Anthony, Duncan 27,
Nathan Kabongo 20,
Paul Samuels 20,
Allan Kabeja 23,
Christian Alozie 24,
Leroy Dias Dos Santos 24,
Simon Smith 21,
Paul Steadman 32,
Nathan Gordon 23

"We put blood, sweat and tears into what we're doing."

Semi-Final

Act: Dressed in military uniform, Flawless gave a spectacular performance inspired by their experience on the show and popular TV show *The A-Team*. Their eye-popping choreography and the energetic music brought the stage alive! The performance ended with an explosive final leap through the air, and Ant and Dec could hardly be heard above the screaming!

"We've got some tricks up our sleeves."

Judges' Reaction: Amanda was glowing with excitement after watching their routine. "Fantastic performance," she told them. Simon said that he thought their routine was utter genius, and praised them for the time and effort that they had poured into chasing their dream. Piers agreed that it had been unbelievable.

Verdict: The audience votes put Flawless through to the final.

Flawless's Reaction: After working every day, putting everything they had into perfecting their act, words could not express how they felt to get such a positive response! Their family was in the audience to support them every step of the way

Final

Flawless were hugely excited and very happy to be in the final. Their dedication and hard work had truly paid off. Now they had to pull something spectacular out of the bag for the ultimate dance-off!

"We're going to seize the opportunity."

In Their Words: "We want to win because we want to show everyone that if you work hard, you can achieve your dream."

Act: In a routine inspired by their dream of fame and fortune, Flawless drew on popular culture to create an electrifying performance full of fun and enthusiasm. From the moment it began, with the comic touch of the newspapers announcing their win, the audience knew they were in for a treat. Flawless put on an effortlessly brilliant show, fusing the legacy of Michael Jackson with slick moves and a hint of New York cool. This was street-dance at its most thrilling!

Judges' Reaction: Simon was full of praise, saying, "From the minute we saw you, you have not put a foot wrong. That was incredible." Piers said it was a scintillating performance, and Amanda told the group that they made her proud to be British because it was "utter perfection".

Flawless's Reaction: Winning this competition would change the lives of the group completely. They put everything they had into their performance, and they were united in their determination to keep chasing their dream!

John Neill, seventy-six, and his twelve-year-old granddaughter Sallie Lax have been singing together for two years. Sallie feels more confident singing with her grandfather, and John loves singing with her.

John has been a singer for over fifty years, and has performed all over the country. He has loved singing since he was a schoolboy, and is delighted that his granddaughter shares his passion for music. John sings in a male-voice choir that has performed in churches, halls and retirement homes.

Together, Sallie and John capture the essence of *Britain's Got Talent*. All over the country, families sit down together and enjoy the show. It is a place where the hidden talents of ordinary people can be celebrated and appreciated. Uniting family and talent, 2 Grand are the perfect *Britain's Got Talent* act!

"Tonight we're going to sing our hearts out and make Britain proud of 2 Grand!"

2 GRAND

"It's the most wonderful thing in the world that's ever happened to us."

Audition

Song: John and Sallie decided to perform A Whole New World for their audition. They walked confidently onto the stage as Sallie's mother waited in the wings with Ant and Dec. Would the audience like their performance? What would the Judges say? Sometimes it's more nerve-wracking to be the supporters.

Sallie's mother need not have worried! The audience responded to the warmth of 2 Grand before they even began to perform! John started to sing, and then Sallie's voice joined his, soaring around the theatre. The audience erupted into applause, instantly responding to John and Sallie. This humble family act brought a magic onto the stage that no one could have expected, and the audience loved them. However, it wasn't just the audience that 2 Grand had to convince. There were boos and shouts as Simon hit his buzzer! As the song ended and the audience roared its approval, everyone was waiting to hear what the Judges would say!

Judges' Reaction: Piers summed it up when he said that 2 Grand are what Britain's Got Talent is all about. He added that they have natural charm. "You surprised me!" said Amanda with a big smile. Even Simon had to admit that he had felt the charm of the act. "I love the relationship between the two of you... it's just a little bit too sweet."

Verdict: The Judges put 2 Grand through to the next round.

2 Grand's Reaction: They could hardly believe that they were one step closer to their dream!

"When I'm with my granddad, I don't think I've ever get nervous."

85023

Semi-Final

Song: For the semi-final, 2 Grand sang Somewhere Out There. Sallie began alone, standing on a balcony above the stage. The audience loved every minute, and the response at the end of the song was fantastic. Sallie looked radiant and they both sang better than ever before, encouraged by the overwhelming support from the audience.

Judges' Reaction: As they stood waiting for the Judges' comments, they both felt amazing. Amanda wiped her eyes and laughed ruefully. "I'm a complete mess," she joked. "What a fantastic performance – well done, both of you." She went on to say how wonderful it was to see two generations onstage together, and she hoped it would inspire more people to come along and audition with

"Every time I sing with Sallie it's fantastic!"

their grandparents! Simon's heart had melted too. "I don't know what's happened to me tonight," he said with a grin. "I really, really like you two. You're not the best singers in the world but you have complete and utter sincerity. It was just brilliant." "I echo what they both said," Piers concluded. "At its heart, this is a family show. You epitomise what this show is truly about – family entertainment!"

Verdict: The Judges chose to put 2 Grand through to the final.

2 Grand's Reaction: At the end of the show, Sallie was in tears – but they were happy tears!

Final

In Their Words: Before his last performance on Britain's Got Talent, John said that getting through to the final was absolutely out of this world. His and Sallie's lives had changed completely. People had stopped them in the street to ask for their autographs and congratulate them on their performances. The nation took 2 Grand to their hearts, and that support gave John and Sallie the courage, confidence and strength to step out onto the glittering stage and give the performance of their lives!

Song: They sang A Whole New World for the final, and clearly enjoyed every minute of it. Sallie looked beautiful in a stunning red dress, but it was their onstage magic that lit up the studio. The audience listened, breathless. Then, as the last note died away, the applause reached a crescendo. Sallie and her grandfather smiled at each other and turned to face the Judges.

Judges' Reaction: Simon spoke first. "I think nerves got the better of you tonight," he said. "I don't think you're going to win, but I don't think you're going to look back and be disappointed. I love you two – I think you're

terrific." Piers was delighted that 2 Grand were part of the biggest final ever. "You've already won just by standing there," he said. Amanda agreed and added, "I think we're just all in love with the pair of you and the fact that you have such a fantastic relationship."

2 Grand's Reaction: Whatever the final results, entering the competition changed John and Sallie's lives. It strengthened their bond and made them feel on top of the world. And that's the real magic of Britain's Got Talent!

"I've met loads of amazing people."

Ten-year-old Hollie Steel started dancing lessons when she was four. She loves to perform and feels completely at home on stage

She works very hard and is always practising singing, dancing or playing the piano. She is completely determined to make her dreams come true!

HOLLIE STEEL

Audition

Song/act: Hollie began by ballet dancing, but when Simon held his hand over his buzzer, she opened her mouth and began to sing.

Judges' Reaction: Amanda said, Hollie was utterly brilliant. "It's just ridiculous how talented you are," she added. Piers said that she was the best child performer he had ever seen.

"I think you've got a fantastic voice," said Simon.

Verdict: The Judges all agreed, Hollie should sail through to the semi-finals!

Hollie's Reaction: Hollie was overjoyed to get through to the next round. More than anything, she wanted the chance to sing in front of the Queen.

Semi-Final

Song: *Edelweiss.*

Judges' Reaction: Simon praised Hollie's bravery in overcoming her stage fright. "You performed it and you nailed the last note – well done, Hollie." Piers predicted that she would be in the final, and Amanda said, "You're such a little professional – congratulations! The most beautiful, innocent, pure voice."

Verdict: The Judges chose to put Hollie through to the final.

Hollie's Reaction:

"This is the biggest night of my life so far!"

FACT FILE

Home town: Accrington, Lancs
Ambition: To be a professional singer
Job: Schoolgirl
Talent: Singer

"When I talk I sound like I'm from Accrington, but when I sing I sound really posh."

Final

In Her Words: "I feel really really happy and I don't want it to stop!"

Song: *Wishing You Were Somehow Here Again.*

Judges' Reaction: Hollie received a standing ovation, the Judges gave their verdict. "You've made half the audience cry tonight!" Piers joked. "That was great. You sang absolutely beautifully."

Amanda agreed, commenting how beautiful Hollie looked. "You were fantastic," said Simon. "You chose a tough song…you handled the big notes brilliantly."

Hollie's Reaction: Hollie couldn't wait for her moment in the spotlight.

"It's really exciting to be in the final!"

Father and son Demetri and Michalakis Andreas (known as Lagi) Demetriou spend all their time together and have a very special bond. They describe their act as two fat versions of Michael Flatley with a Greek element!

Demetri says, "In a Greek family it's all about being close and family's really important. One part of Greek culture is dancing. I used to own a Greek restaurant and we'd smash a few plates and dance the night away."

Lagi adds, "I would go to my dad's restaurant and see him dancing, and the passion he had made me really want to be up there. My dad means the world to me."

STAVROS FLATLEY

"We've had the best time ever – we've been recognised everywhere!"

Audition

Act: As soon as Lagi and his father stepped onto the stage, the audience warmed to them and to their relationship. After a few words of introduction, they stepped offstage to prepare for their act. The Judges sat quietly; it was clear that they weren't expecting to be amazed. Then the music began, and a husky voice echoed around the theatre. "Ladies and gentlemen, many years ago in Cyprus lived a man who loved to dance. He would dance for the villagers, and the villagers loved to watch him dance. Well, ladies and gentleman, tonight, here for one night only, would you please welcome Mr Stavros Flatley."

Demetri burst out from the wings and the audience roared with laughter and delight at the sight of his short trousers, bare chest and blonde wig. He leapt around the stage, switching from Greek to Irish dancing in the blink of an eye. Simon and Piers grinned, and Amanda threw back her head and howled with laughter.

It seemed as if the act couldn't get any funnier and the cheers couldn't get any louder. But then Lagi danced onstage, a miniature version of his father. The crowd went crazy!

No one wanted the dancing to stop, but Demetri and Lagi finished with a flourish, throwing their blond wigs into the audience! Simon caught one of the wigs and

passed it to Piers, who willingly put it on. The whoops, whistles and applause were deafening! Even Ant and Dec were cheering from the wings.

Judges' Reaction: "I'm ecstatic!" beamed Amanda. "What's Greek for 'yes'?" Simon said, "This is one of my favourite ever dance acts, and you two have the most fantastic relationship." Piers added, "I found your act incredibly entertaining."

Verdict: The Judges put Stavros Flatley straight through to the next round!

Stavros Flatley's Reaction: They were delighted to have made it through to the next round, and were determined to put on another fantastic show.

"There isn't anybody else on this earth I'd rather share a stage with."

FACT FILE

Home town:
North London

Job: Electrical
company director
and student

Talent: Comedy
dancers

"The thing I most enjoy is just spending time with my dad!"

Semi Final

Act: For the semi-final, Demetri and Lagi were determined to give the audience and the Judges something different – something that would blow them away! As the music started and the audience began to clap in time, Demetri appeared in traditional costume – although he was still wearing his trademark blond wig! His charisma and natural sense of comedy soon had everyone laughing.

When Lagi appeared behind him in the same costume, everyone knew they were in for a treat! They danced in perfect time together and then the stage opened up to reveal four backing dancers – old friends of the family!

The music became faster and faster and the performers used the whole stage, sending the audience into gales of laughter. The fantastic relationship between father and son radiated from the stage.

At last the blond wigs were again thrown into the crowd. Stavros Flatley awaited the Judges comments as the audience gave them a standing ovation!

Judges' Reaction: Amanda was beaming. "I just love, love, love, love, love you!" she cried. "I think you're great dancers – you're very, very funny. I just love that you're family . . . it's just what this show's all about."

Piers agreed wholeheartedly, chuckling at the thought of Stavros Flatley entertaining the Queen. Simon added, "It's incredibly infectious and I think the final would be a worse place without you two there."

Verdict: The public voted Stavros Flatley through to the next round.

Stavros Flatley's Reaction: Demetri took the time to thank his son for dancing with him in front of the nation. "I've had the time of my life," he said.

Final

In Their Words: "I can't believe that we're in the final," said Demetri. "Here we are, two little podgy fellows, and the public have picked up their phones and voted for us. How cool is that?"

Act: Ant and Dec introduced Stavros Flatley as the duo who always puts a smile on everyone's face. Their family was bursting with pride to see them perform on the final of Britain's Got Talent. Lagi and Demetri promised "more moves, more attitude and more belly", and they were true to their word! Their comic timing drew roars of laughter from the audience, who were already on their feet when

"This is the biggest thing that's ever happened to us."

a troupe of Irish dancers joined Stavros Flatley onstage.

Judges' Reaction: The audience and the Judges were united in adoring the performance. "You are my favourite act!" Amanda admitted with glee. "You've been my secret favourites right the way along. I want you to win the show!" "I thought it was absolute, utter genius," said Simon. "You make people feel good . . . it

has been an absolute privilege and honour having you two on the show." With the blond wig perched on his head, Piers added, "It would be absolutely hilarious if you two perform on the Royal

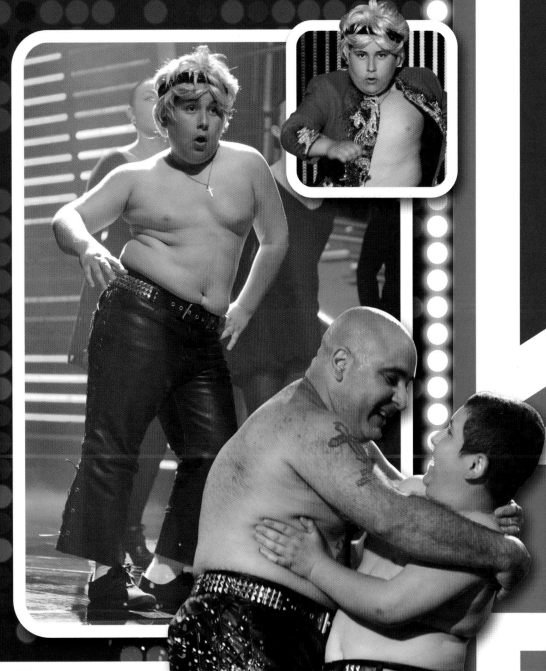

Variety Performance in front of the Queen." The applause from the crowd was deafening!

Stavros Flatley's Reaction: "The feeling that we get when we're doing it together is the best," said Demetri. "You look around and he's there." Demetri and Lagi's fantastic relationship is what Britain's Got Talent is all about!

"I look up to my dad so much; he's just a role model for me."

Shaheen lives in Swansea with his mum and his cat. He had his first singing lesson when he was seven and goes to stage school every Saturday. Shaheen loves performing and can often be found on the stage at local charity shows and school plays. Singing means everything to him, and he is determined that it will play a major role in his life.

"This is how one song can change your life."

SHAHEEN JAFARGHOLI

"When I start singing, my whole body just beams as bright as a light."

Audition

Song: Shaheen began by singing Valerie, but Simon stopped him almost as soon as he had started! In the wings, Shaheen's mum looked on in nervous alarm. What had gone wrong? Simon said that he didn't think the song was right, and asked whether Shaheen had prepared anything else. There was a long silence, and then Shaheen swallowed his nerves and nodded. He began to sing Who's Loving You? . . . and he brought the house down!

Judges' Reaction: Simon was beaming – he knew that he had been right to change Shaheen's song! He said that this could be the start of something special for Shaheen. "You have just shown that Wales has got talent," Piers told him. Amanda got goosebumps when she listened

"You have just shown that Wales has got talent,"

to Shaheen singing!

Verdict: Shaheen went through to the next round with three yesses!

Shaheen's Reaction: He couldn't believe that his singing had brought the Judges to their feet. It was a moment he will remember for the rest of his life!

FACT FILE

Home town: Swansea
Ambition: To be a singer
Job: Schoolboy
Talent: Singer

"I can't believe what happened to me!"

Semi-Final

Song: Everyone was wondering whether Shaheen could deliver as impressive a performance second time around. When he announced that he was going to sing And I Am Telling You I'm Not Going, Simon raised his eyebrows. That's a tough song to get right! Whatever the Judges' worries, Shaheen looked completely relaxed up on stage. He handled the pressure of the semi-final with ease, and as he belted out his song it was clear that the audience loved him.

Judges' Reaction: Piers found Shaheen's performance "breathtaking to watch" and

said that it was the best singing performance in the semi-finals so far. Amanda lavished praised on him, and Simon said that he was a real contender to win the competition.

Verdict: In a nail-biting conclusion to the show, Shaheen was put through to the final by the Judges.

Shaheen's Reaction: Shaheen was overwhelmed. "It was so amazing!" he gasped.

"You have absolute star quality."

Final

In His Words: "For me, it gets better every round!"

Song: Shaheen delivered a fantastic version of his landmark audition song, Who's Loving You? The crowd warmed instantly to his open-hearted nature, and it was obvious to everyone that this lad from Wales belonged in the spotlight!

Judges' Reaction: "Absolutely unbelievable!" said Piers. "That was an incredible performance." Amanda said, "I can just tell you completely love what you're doing. You have absolute star quality." Simon was full of praise. "I think you're a super, super talented young man," he said. "You're in with a real shot here, Shaheen."

Shaheen's Reaction: Shaheen loved every moment of his time on the show.

"It means so much to be here in the final!"

SUSAN BOYLE

"I just want the chance to perform in front of the Queen."

Church volunteer Susan Boyle comes from West Lothian in Scotland. She lives at home with her cat Pebbles and has been singing since she was twelve years old. Her cheeky sense of humour is irrepressible, and although she is shy, she has always wanted to perform in front of a large audience.

"I'm going to make that audience rock!"

She took singing lessons from a voice coach, attended Edinburgh Acting School and has taken part in the Edinburgh Fringe. But before her audition for *Britain's Got Talent*, Susan's main experience of singing in front of an audience was in church . . . as well as a bit of karaoke!

Susan won a number of local singing competitions and her mother urged her to enter *Britain's Got Talent*. When her mother died she decided to audition.

Audition

When Ant and Dec interviewed a reserved lady in a cream dress at the Glasgow auditions, they had no idea that her name would soon be known all around the world! Ant and Dec reassured her as she admitted that she felt a little nervous. Then Susan Boyle walked onto the stage, clutching her microphone in her hand.

It was clear that the Judges and the audience had already made up their minds about her. "What's the dream?" asked Simon. Susan's answer was simple: "I'm trying to be a professional singer." When she added that she would like to be as successful a singer as Elaine Paige, there were giggles from the audience. Piers couldn't repress a chuckle. Susan announced that she was going to sing *I Dreamed a Dream* from *Les Miserables* and people in the audience exchanged doubtful looks. Everyone thought this was going to be a funny audition. Simon rolled his eyes and asked her to start when she was ready.

The music started softly and Susan waited calmly for her cue. She smiled at the Judges, and then she opened her mouth and started to sing.

Home town:
Blackburn,
West Lothian
Ambition: To be
as successful as
Elaine Paige
Job: Church
volunteer
Talent: Singer

"Being on *Britain's Got Talent* is a chance to turn my life around and fulfil the dream."

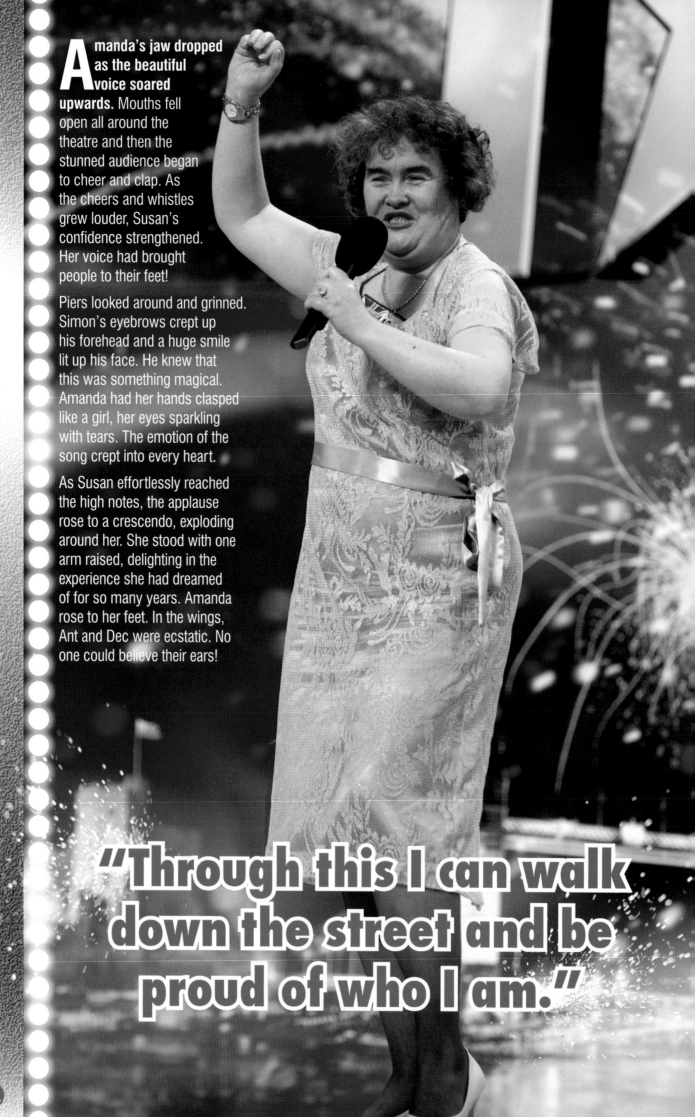

Amanda's jaw dropped as the beautiful voice soared upwards. Mouths fell open all around the theatre and then the stunned audience began to cheer and clap. As the cheers and whistles grew louder, Susan's confidence strengthened. Her voice had brought people to their feet!

Piers looked around and grinned. Simon's eyebrows crept up his forehead and a huge smile lit up his face. He knew that this was something magical. Amanda had her hands clasped like a girl, her eyes sparkling with tears. The emotion of the song crept into every heart.

As Susan effortlessly reached the high notes, the applause rose to a crescendo, exploding around her. She stood with one arm raised, delighting in the experience she had dreamed of for so many years. Amanda rose to her feet. In the wings, Ant and Dec were ecstatic. No one could believe their ears!

"Through this I can walk down the street and be proud of who I am."

The final bars of the song rang out and Susan blew a kiss to the audience. It was time to find out what the Judges thought. Piers began by saying, "That was the biggest surprise I have had in three years of this show. When you stood there with that cheeky grin and said that you wanted to be like Elaine Paige, everyone was laughing at you. No one is laughing now. That was stunning – an incredible performance. Amazing – I'm reeling from shock."

"I am so thrilled because I know that everybody was against you," said Amanda. "It was a complete privilege listening to that."

Simon made everyone laugh when he said, "Susan, I knew the minute you walked out on that stage that we were going to hear something extraordinary, and I was right."

"What a lot of tosh!" chuckled Dec, knowing that Simon had been as surprised as everyone else.

It was the moment of truth – would Susan go through to the semi-finals?

"The biggest yes I have ever given anyone," said Piers.

"Yes, definitely," said Amanda.

"It's three yesses!" said Simon.

Susan danced with joy! Ant and Dec were waiting for her as she walked into the wings, feeling absolutely fantastic. But no one had any idea of how famous Susan was about to become.

Semi-Final

By the time of the semi-final, Susan Boyle's name was known worldwide. Her impact had been phenomenal. Everyone was expecting a spectacular performance, and the pressure on Susan was immense.

She walked onto the stage as the music for *Memory* began to play. The Judges' hearts were in their mouths. Would she be able to conquer her nerves and give the performance that would get her through to the final?

Her voice wobbled as she began to sing, but like a true professional she controlled it. The audience was breathless – willing her to succeed as they listened to the words echoing around the studio.

Small and solitary on the stage, Susan held the audience captivated. As she hit the quivering last note of the song, the crowd whistled, shouted and roared their approval.

"You sang beautifully," said Piers. "Thank you, Susan."

"I am just so relieved that it went so fantastically well for you," said Amanda with a dazzling smile. "You nailed that performance. I am so proud of you and I'm proud that you represented Britain so brilliantly."

"You are one special lady," said Simon. "I just want to

apologise because of the way we treated you before you sang the first time. You've made me and everyone else look very stupid. I'm very happy for you and very proud of you."

The last few weeks had been like a dream for Susan. When she was told that the audience had voted her through to the final, she could hardly believe her ears.

"I've enjoyed every second and I'll do it again."

75

Final

For the final, Susan chose to sing *I Dreamed A Dream* – the performance that had been seen around the world and had made her a star. The pressure of the week leading up to the final was overwhelming, and the Judges felt astounded that she had coped with it as well as she had.

"It's the most important night of my life tonight," Susan said simply. "When I step on that stage it's an accumulation of forty years of dreaming. A life-long ambition."

Looking elegant in a long dress, Susan stepped onto the stage, feeling completely at home. Starry lights twinkled behind her and the atmosphere was magical. She sang from the heart, performing with perfect control. At the end of the song, the response from the crowd was deafening. Everyone had loved it.

"All my life I have striven to prove myself - that I'm not the worthless person that some people think I am; that I do have something to offer."

The Judges smiled. "That, to me, was the greatest performance I've seen in *Britain's Got Talent* history," said Piers.

"I have never heard such powerful, confident vocals," added Amanda.

Simon praised Susan's courage in performing despite her critics, and said that she could hold her head high.

As she stood beside Ant and Dec, Susan thanked everyone for their support. In just a few weeks, this shy lady from Scotland had become one of the best-known people on the planet. Whatever happened next, one thing was certain. Susan Boyle's life would never be the same again.

WHAT'S NEXT?

The internet has helped to make Susan a star around the world, and her career as a singer is only just beginning. The audience took her to their hearts, and her forthcoming album will no doubt have many eager fans. *Britain's Got Talent* is all about opportunity. Susan Boyle seized that opportunity with both hands, and she will always stand as one of the show's most wonderful and memorable surprises.

"I want to thank people for all the support they've given me."

Twelve-year-old Aidan Davis is a body-popper who has only been dancing for six months. He taught himself using the TV and the internet! He is a passionate dancer who puts a huge amount of time and effort into improving his moves and skills. Aidan's love of dance is his driving force, and he lights up the stage with his energy and enthusiasm!

"This opportunity means the world to me."

AIDAN DAVIS

"I love dancing so much."

Audition

Act: Aidan looked very humble as he stood in front of the Judges and simply told them "I just like dancing". But as soon as the music started, his body-popping dance routine had the audience cheering and the Judges gasping in amazement. His fluid movements and his utter confidence made him a joy to watch.

Judges' Reaction: Piers said that he thought Aidan was just as good as George Sampson, the previous year's winner. Amanda agreed and said that Aidan had raised the bar. "I think you're better than any dancer I've ever seen on this show," said Simon. "You are super, super, super talented." He was astounded to learn that Aidan had worked out the routine himself.

In the wings, Aidan's mother was over the moon. "We've never had three 'supers' before!" Dec told her.

Verdict: The Judges gladly put Aidan through to the semi-finals!

Aidan's Reaction: Aidan enjoyed performing, but he could hardly believe the wonderful reaction he got!

Home town: Birmingham

Ambition: To make dancing his career

Job: Schoolboy

Talent: Dancer

"My dream would be to dance at the Royal Variety in front of the Queen."

Semi-Final

Act: Performing in the semi-final was the biggest thing Aidan had ever done. He had been sensational in his first audition, but now he had to be even better. Could he pull it off? Aidan performed his routine in front of mirrored images of himself, and made his complicated moves look simple. The audience loved every minute of it!

Judges' Reaction: Amanda was blown away by Aidan's performance. "Your audition was unbelievable – I didn't really think you could top it," she said. "But you just . . . went through the roof!"

"Whatever 'it' is, you've got 'it'," said Simon. "Total confidence, total charisma, great face, great routine."

"You have got something very special," Piers added, "It's a delight to watch you."

Verdict: Aidan could not stop smiling after his performance. He had hardly expected the reactions to be better than at his first auditions. "That was absolutely amazing and the response is just incredible!" he said. When he heard that he was going through to the final, his knees gave way underneath him. He was one step closer to the Royal Varie

Aidan's Reaction: Aidan coul not stop smiling after his performance. He had hardly expected the reactions to be better than at his first auditior "That was absolutely amazing and the response is just incredible!" he said. When he heard that he was going throu to the final, his knees gave wa underneath him. He was one step closer to the Royal Varie

Final

Aidan only had twenty-four hours after winning the semi-final to prepare for his performance in the final! He spent as much time practising as he could. He knew that he was going to be up against all the best acts from the show, and he had to throw his heart and soul into this last performance.

In His Words: "I'm going to go out there and try my hardest and do my best!"

Act: Aidan's routine for the final was performed on a moving floor and enhanced by flickering lights and a glimmering spotlight. The audience reaction was spectacular, and it was clear that Aidan loved every second of it. Best of all, his proud parents were watching and loving every moment.

"I have to dance better than I've ever danced before."

Judges' Reaction: Amanda beamed as she congratulated Aidan on his genius dancing and said that she loved his attitude. "You're so relaxed you're a joy to watch," she said. "You're a superstar waiting to happen."

Simon shocked the audience by saying, "It wasn't as good as last night . . . but whatever happens you've got a huge future ahead of you." But Piers disagreed with Simon. He thought it was a brilliant performance, and reminded the audience that Aidan had taught himself to dance. "You are brilliant at what you do," he said.

Aidan's Reaction: "I loved it!" gasped Aidan, as he thanked everyone who voted him through to the final. The audience cheered as he waved to them, and a hopeful smile lit up his face. Could he be the winner of *Britain's Got Talent* 2009?

Diversity is made up of eleven lads from East London and Essex aged between thirteen and twenty-five.

DIVERSITY

The group includes three sets of brothers and four friends. They have known each other since they were very young, so their fantastic onstage chemistry is based on real friendship. Just like lots of people all over the country, their talent started out as a group of friends having fun!

Some of the younger members of the group are still at school or university, but among the older members are a bathroom installer and an IT systems engineer. They may be from different walks of life, but dance is what brings them together.

Ashley is the group's choreographer, and he works tirelessly to create exciting routines, using films and modern culture for inspiration. He has been teaching himself routines since the age of fourteen, and he fits in his choreography around his Natural Science degree studies at university!

"Who dares wins."

FACT FILE

Names:

Ashley Banjo 20

Jordan Banjo 16

Ian McNaughton 25

Jamie McNaughton 23

Matthew
McNaughton 16

Mitchell Craske 12

Sam Craske 19

Warren Russell 18

Terry Smith 24

Perri Luc Kiely 13

Ike Ezekwugo 22

Audition

Standing in the wings and waiting to audition, the boys chatted to Ant and Dec about their dream of performing at the Royal Variety Performance. "There's not really a much bigger show to do," said Ashley. Their moment arrived and the dancers walked onto the stage to face the Judges. No one paid much attention to the large black bag they placed at the back of the stage.

The boys got into position and waited for the music to start. In their black outfits with their hoods up, they looked good – but could their performance match up to their looks?

Of course it could! Their imaginative routine had the audience cheering, and when one of the youngest dancers burst out of the mysterious black bag, there was a roar of approval. Their slow-motion race to the finish line drew whoops from the crowd, and their back flips and high jumps astonished everyone.

At the end of the routine, the audience erupted with applause, cheers and whistles. Simon could be seen mouthing "Brilliant", and in the wings Ant and Dec were clapping and grinning.

Diversity got three HUGE yesses!

Their families and friends were waiting backstage to greet them and hear the good news. They were through to the next round.

Decision Time

When the moment came to decide which acts would make it to the final, the three Judges had some tough decisions to make.

The standard of dancers this year has been higher than we've ever had," Simon told Diversity and fellow dance group Flawless. "A lot of very, very good dancers are not going to make it through." He paused, waiting for this statement to sink in, before grinning and adding casually, "You're in the semi-finals!"

The dancers went crazy with excitement!

85

Semi-Final

Diversity had the honour – and the terror! – of opening the semi- finals. They knew that their performance had to dazzle the audience, and they were determined to challenge themselves with some truly difficult moves.

It was an awesome performance. Perri was flung across the stage with perfect timing, but before the audience could recover from that move, Mitchell was lowered down from the ceiling – Mission Impossible style!

Every time it seemed as if the routine couldn't get any better, the lads pulled another incredible stunt out of the bag! It had the perfect comic touch too – everyone laughed when they mimed voting for themselves! As the music finished with the words, "Stage one complete", the applause was deafening.

The Judges gave the performers a standing ovation. "You lot were fantastic tonight," said Piers.

"We just want to give it our all!"

"It was intelligent, innovative and so funny," Amanda told the group. "I can't take my eyes off you when I'm watching you... utterly, utterly fantastic."

"I genuinely didn't think you'd improve on what I saw first time round, but you did," said Simon. "Sensational – congratulations.

It was left up to the Judges to decide who would go through to the final – Diversity or Natalie Okri. It was a tough decision!

Piers said, "I'm going to go with the act that I think genuinely stands the best chance of winning the whole competition and that is... Diversity."

Amanda said, "Both these acts are in my top three. The act that I am going to put through this evening is... Natalie."

Simon was left with the casting vote. He said, "I am going to agree with Piers."

There were a lot of nerves and a lot of expectations before Diversity's final performance on *Britain's Got Talent*.

"It feels amazing to be in the final," said Ashley. "I can't believe we've actually got this far. To be doing this with my brother and all my best mates is the best feeling in the world. If we win tonight it would allow us to do what we love doing full-time instead of part-time with the people closest to us."

But the question on everyone's lips was – how could it get any better? "They've done so many incredible performances," said Simon. "How do they top it for the final?"

"It feels amazing to be in the final."

Final

From the moment that their final routine began and they transformed themselves into a single robotic giant, it was clear that Diversity had something very special for the audience They leapt around the stage as if they were made of rubber! Inspired by blockbuster movies like *Transformers* and *Superman*, the performance drew gasps of astonishment and incredulity from the crowd. They moved as fluidly as a single unit, making their complicated moves look effortless. Their parody of the *Britain's Got Talent* show was a comic masterpiece!

With one final elastic back flip from Perri, the act came to an end. All around the studio and all around the country, people were on their feet, applauding and cheering.

"To come this far and to get a response like that – I can't thank everyone enough," said Ashley.

"Your choreography is second to none."

"You have practically rendered me speechless, Ashley," said Amanda. "Your choreography is second to none."

"If I had to give marks on that, this would be the only performance tonight I would give a ten to," said Simon, "There was not a step out of place. It was sheer and utter perfection."

"I thought it was a fantastic performance," said Piers.

But it wasn't up to the Judges – it was up to the viewers at home to cast their votes, and millions of people rang the show. At last, after five dramatic semi-finals and the biggest final ever, one act was about to win a place on the bill at the Royal Variety Performance.

"The winner of Britain's Got Talent 2009 is... Diversity!"

WHAT HAPPENS NEXT?

As well as coping with a whirlwind of TV and newspaper interviews, live performances and star appearances, Diversity has taken part in the *Britain's Got Talent* tour with the nine other finalists. The dance troupe is also going to appear in a new film, which will be shot in 3D. Flawless will also appear in the film, alongside 2008's *Britain's Got Talent* winner George Sampson.

The most exciting event on the horizon is, of course, their chance to perform before the Queen at the Royal Variety Performance in December. Ashley promises that they are going to work very hard to produce an amazing routine for the show!

There are many, many other exciting moments to come for the boys! After the final Simon said, "What you just saw tonight was one of the greatest performances I've ever seen on any talent show." No one who has seen them perform could argue with that!

Somewhere out there is the winner of *Britain's Got Talent* 2010! Could it be you? Do you have a passion for dance like Diversity? Can you sing like an angel? Perhaps you can do magic, impressions, staggering stunts or amazing acrobatics.

Whatever your talent, don't keep it to yourself. Listen out for the announcement of the 2010 auditions. This is your opportunity to reach for the stars!

WINNER?

PAUL POTTS

"This competition has been the best thing that's ever happened to me."

Paul Potts grew up in Bristol, and developed his love of singing at school. Although he was bullied, his singing was almost a great comfort to him. He sang in several choirs and performed in a number of amateur operatic productions.

In 2003 Paul had a bad bike accident, which stopped him from pursuing a music career. When he decided to audition for *Britain's Got Talent*, he was working as a mobile phone salesman and he hadn't sung onstage for years.

"I've always wanted to sing as a career."

Audition

When Paul arrived for his first audition, his confidence was at rock bottom. He looked uncomfortable onstage and it was clear that the Judges weren't expecting much. But when he began to sing *Nessun Dorma*, everyone was stunned and delighted. Simon's mouth fell open and Amanda wiped her tears away. His voice was wonderful!

"I wasn't expecting that, Paul," said Simon. "This was a complete breath of fresh air."

Paul's face lit up as Piers added, "You have an incredible voice." They unanimously voted him through to the next round.

Paul was happy but shocked – the reaction had been so wonderful!

Final

After sailing through the semi-final, Paul arrived at the final to sing *Nessun Dorma* again. He gave a staggering performance, and the audience reaction was everything he could have hoped for. He couldn't believe that this was happening to him!

Piers said, "I've just seen the winner of *Britain's*

Got Talent." Amanda echoed Piers' comments, and Simon added, "I'd love you to win after that performance."

When Dec announced that Paul was the winner, Paul's hands flew to his mouth in shock. "Thank you for believing in me," he told viewers.

The Prize

Paul Potts won his dream prize – to perform at the Royal Variety Performance. Simon, Amanda and Piers came onstage first to introduce him. Simon recalled how he had sighed when at the auditions "a very nervous-looking mobile-phone salesman shuffled onto the stage". But he and the other Judges had been proved wrong.

Paul's performance of *Nella Fantasia* and *Nessun Dorma* held the audience spellbound, and they erupted when he finished!

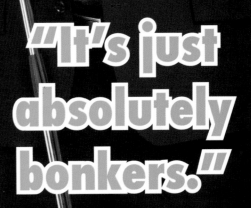

"It's just absolutely bonkers."

The Prime Minister is a Paul Potts fan!

LIFE AFTER BRITAIN'S GOT TALENT

Winning *Britain's Got Talent* helped Paul to believe in himself again – it was a truly life-changing moment. Since that time, all his dreams of becoming a professional singer have come true.

In 2007, he released his first album *One Chance*. It reached number one in ten countries and his second album, *Passione*, was released in June 2009. Paul has performed onstage and on TV many times across the world in concerts and on TV shows – and he doesn't work as a mobile phone salesman any more!

★★★☆ PAST WINNER PROFILE ★★★★
GEORGE SAMPSON

"I know this competition is everything."

George Sampson is a street dancer from Warrington and, like Paul Potts, he got his big chance on *Britain's Got Talent*. George first auditioned in 2007 and did well, but didn't quite make it through to the semi-finals. He spent the following year training as hard as he could to improve, and he came back in 2008 hoping that this time he would be lucky.

Audition

He came nervously onstage . . . and wowed the crowd! In the wings, Ant and Dec were willing him to do well. "He's wicked!" Dec exclaimed as he watched the routine. The audience loved George's act and the Judges were all grinning.

"I thought you were phenomenal!" said Simon. "The best dancer we have had by a clear mile." Amanda thought he was really cool, and Piers agreed. The Judges gladly gave him three yesses!

"I'm really over the moon at the moment," George said when he got through to the semi-finals. He could hardly believe that he was one step closer to fulfilling his dream.

"I just really want to be a dancer."

Final

George's *Singing In the Rain* dance at the final stunned the crowd. He was determined to battle in order to change his life for the better, and his passion for dance shone out of him. His performance had the crowd on their feet, cheering and whooping. The Judges were just as excited as the audience!

"You've got a great chance," said Piers. Amanda beamed and said, "That was a winning routine." Simon, "On sheer determination, George, you've got to have a chance of winning the competition after that."

Simon was right, of course! When Ant announced that George had won, he grabbed his head and did a spin on the spot – he simply couldn't believe his ears!

The Prize

George's act at the Royal Variety Performance began with his silhouette, and then he appeared in a sparkling burst of light. His routine was dazzling, and George's control and style was even more polished than when he performed on *Britain's Got Talent*. He truly surpassed himself!

"I've been dancing on the streets of Manchester just to get better!"

LIFE AFTER *BRITAIN'S GOT TALENT*

Since winning *Britain's Got Talent*, George's life has been like a dream come true. He has made his West End stage debut in a hip-hop musical, released a DVD and performed for the crowds at a Rugby League match, as well as helping to promote a number of products and becoming a patron of a children's charity. He has a huge fan base and still cannot quite believe that he is allowed to dance for a living. George's journey has been incredible, but it has only just begun!

STEPHEN MULHERN

Stephen Mulhern is a hugely popular presenter and loves presenting *Britain's Got More Talent*. He really enjoys seeing all the weird and wonderful talents that the country has to offer!

Stephen started entertaining when he was a boy, and has always loved comedy and magic. His parents were market traders, and Stephen worked on the stall when he was a teenager, learning how to entertain the customers. He soon picked up the tricks of the trade, and – even more importantly – he discovered how much he liked an audience!

One of the things that Stephen loves about *Britain's Got Talent* is that it's the kind of entertainment that the whole family can enjoy together. He also understands the dreams of the contestants having got his big break on a TV talent show, he can tell them first hand how it feels to perform in front of the Queen!

"The auditions are in town!"

Stephen began his presenting career working on various kids TV shows and has even won a Bafta. As well as hosting *Animals Do The Funniest Things for ITV1* and *Britain's Got More Talent for ITV2*, Stephen has worked on a huge variety of stage shows and even toured with his own one man variety show. The highlight of his stage career was being invited to appear on The Royal Variety Performance in front of the Queen and the Duke of Edinburgh!

"Makes you proud to be British!"

"The ITV2 interviews know no boundaries!"

FACT FILE

Full name: Stephen Daniel Mulhern

Birthday: April 4th, 1977

Birthplace: Stratford

Role model: Michael Crawford

Favourite act: Stavros Flatley

BRITAIN'S GOT EVEN MORE

FACES OF DISCO

Faces of Disco got some of the biggest cheers of the night when they performed at the semi-finals. Their high-energy, fun-filled routine had people dancing in the aisles! Their dream is to give up the day jobs and become full-time entertainers.

FAMOUS FACES

PINT-SIZED POPSTAR

NATALIE OKRI

Natalie loves singing and wants to be a diva like Beyonce! She sings all the time, and this was her chance to share her passion with the country. She gave an awesome performance at her audition, without a trace of nerves!

T★LENT

A selection of our favourite moments from series three!

BRITAIN'S GOT EVEN MORE

FRED BOWERS

FAVE PENSIONER

Fred has been breakdancing for five years and dances every night of the week. He loves it, and the fact that he's seventy-three years old doesn't hold him back one bit!

JULIA NAIDENKO

Julia Naidenko entranced the judges and the audience with her slinky shimmies. There were cheers of appreciation from the crowd as she descended to the stage on a swing and performed her dazzling routine.

BEST BELLY

T★LENT

A selection of our favourite moments from series three

BRITAIN'S GOT
EVEN MORE

MAMMA TRISH

BEST DRAG QUEEN

Pete from Birmingham has been an entertainer for twenty-six years. But he's never had an audience like the *Britain's Got Talent* crowd!

MIKE
HENDERSON

Mike is a retired swimming pool manager – and his talent is to do a handstand on knives. Amanda could hardly bear to watch! But he certainly had the audience on a knife's edge . . .

T★LENT

A selection of our favourite moments from series three!

BRITAIN'S GOT EVEN MORE

THE BARROW BOYS

FAVE FARMERS

After watching the Barrow Boys, no one will ever look at wheelbarrows in the same way again. Their onstage acrobatics lit up the stage – even if Piers and Simon didn't like the act!

DJ TALENT

Anthony Ghosh is the King of Bling from south London, who rapped his way into the semi-finals. Noted for his £7,000 gold teeth!

BEST BLING

T★LENT

A selection of our favourite moments from series three!

BRITAIN'S GOT EVEN MORE

CALLUM FRANCIS

Callum loves singing and dancing, and he practises everywhere he can – even the bathroom! Callum's parents are immensely proud of him, and he's bursting with talent. This is his chance in the spotlight!

FAVOURITE WEST END WONDER

SUPERMAN!

MANJIT SINGH

Manjit's strength staggered the Judges and amazed the audience. No one could believe the sight of him blowing up the hot-water bottle. But when he pulled a truck with just one ear, there was spontaneous applause!

T★LENT

A selection of our favourite moments from series three!